TRAINER'S

Pocketfile

of Ready-To-Use **Activities**

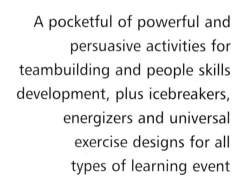

A pocketful of powerful and
persuasive activities for
teambuilding and people skills
development, plus icebreakers,
energizers and universal
exercise designs for all
types of learning event

John Townsend

Published by:

MANAGEMENT POCKETBOOKS

Management Pocketbooks Ltd
Laurel House
Station Approach
Alresford
Hants
SO24 9JH
U.K.

Tel: +44 (0)1962 735573
Fax: +44 (0)1962 733637
E-mail: sales@pocketbook.co.uk
Website: www.pocketbook.co.uk

First published in 1997 as The Trainer's Red Pocketfile of ready-to-use exercises. This edition published in 2005.

ISBN 1 903776 39 2

British Library Cataloguing-in-Publication Data – A catalogue record for this book is available from the British Library.

Design, typesetting and graphics by **efex ltd**. Printed in the UK.

CONTENTS

ICEBREAKERS & ENERGIZERS   5
Autographs   7
Job titles   9
Astro icebreaker   11
Euromorn   18
'Icebreaker' icebreaker   29
Whose shoes?   31
Hexaslogans   34
Tell-tale objects   36

UNIVERSAL EXERCISE DESIGNS   37
Jigsaw learning   38
Musical walls   40
Force field analysis   41
Detective enquiry   44
Role debate   45
Dividing participants into small groups   46

7 WONDERS   49
CONSENSUS-SEEKING
Description and objectives, trainer's guide,
trainer's review guide and tips, exercise

TERRA NOVA   57
LEADERSHIP & PLANNING
Description and objectives, trainer's guide,
suggested options, trainer's review guide
and tips, exercise

VIKING ATTACK!   83
TEAMBUILDING
Description and objectives, trainer's guide,
solution, trainer's review guide, exercise

HOW TO USE THE CD

To undertake the activities in this Pocketfile you will, in most cases, need to prepare participant handouts. Instructions on doing so can be found in this book, at the beginning of each of the applicable activities.

To help you prepare professional-looking handouts we have bundled with this Pocketfile a CD ROM which contains the Team Instruction Cards, Maps, Clue Cards and other materials required for the activities. Look out for this logo:

Simply insert the CD in your disc drive and, on a **PC**, it should automatically start. If this is not the case, access the CD via Windows Explorer or File Manager. On **Apple Macs** access the CD via your desktop and double click on the Red-pocketfile icon.

With the CD loaded, click on the relevant chapter or activity to find the images you wish to print off.

We recommend that you print from your laser or inkjet printer on to fairly thick paper of about 160 gsm. Such paper is available in a range of colours, so you can give each of your participating teams a set of handouts in a different colour.

Often there will be two or more images to an A4 page so have some scissors or a retractable knife handy in order to trim the cards to size (follow the trim guidelines printed on the page).

If your PC crashes and you're in a hurry, don't panic because you can photocopy the handouts from the pages of this book!

1CEBREAKERS & ENERGIZERS

ICEBREAKERS & ENERGIZERS
ABOUT THIS SECTION

The following activities can be used as:

- **Icebreakers** at the beginning of a course to get things off to a good start, accelerate trainee participation and make sure everyone feels included (sometimes called *inclusion activities*) or as…

- **Energizers** at any time during a training course when you feel that the energy level in the room is dropping, people are losing concentration or that the group's cohesion is not what it should be.

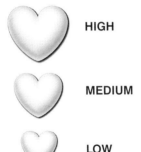

HIGH

MEDIUM

LOW

I have classified each activity as being high, medium or low *effect*. In other words, how much *heart* (self-revelation) does the exercise ask of participants? How embarrassing might it be for someone to participate? You should choose an icebreaker/energizer which has a heart level that fits with the amount of self-revelation which will be required of participants during the rest of the course.

ICEBREAKERS & ENERGIZERS

AUTOGRAPHS

MEDIUM

■ Here's a ready-made 'classic' for you to use on your very next course!

1. Print as many copies of the Autographs card (illustrated overleaf) as there are participants on the course.

2. Distribute a card to each participant and ask them to write their name in the top left hand corner.

3. Explain that they are to visit each of their fellow participants and find eight **different** people who, by signing their autograph next to one of the eight statements, agree that it applies to them. In other words, they must obtain the signature of one person who has blue eyes, another person who looks younger than his or her age, another who has recently travelled to a foreign country, etc, etc.

4. Award a prize to the first (or last!) person to finish.

Autographs

NAME	
HAS RECENTLY TRAVELLED TO A FOREIGN COUNTRY	
LOOKS FRIENDLY TO ME	
BORN UNDER MY ASTROLOGICAL SIGN	
HAS BEEN IN PRESENT JOB MORE THAN ONE YEAR	
HAS AN UNUSUAL HOBBY	
HAS BLUE EYES	
PLAYS A MUSICAL INSTRUMENT	
LOOKS YOUNGER THAN HIS/HER AGE	

ICEBREAKERS & ENERGIZERS
JOB TITLES

LOW

■ A 'safe' icebreaker for trainers who are (wrongly!) worried that adults don't like playing games. Especially suited to management seminars.

1. Print as many copies of the Job Titles card (overleaf) as there are participants.

2. Distribute one card to each participant.

3. Ask them to circulate around the room (cocktail-party fashion) to interview each of the other participants and obtain the three basic pieces of information: Name, Job Title, Number of Reports.

4. When they have all finished, you can use the information in a number of ways:

    ● Check that everyone has the same total number in the bottom right hand corner; if not, you can have some jolly repartee as to why not!

    ● Underline the importance of leadership skills when the participant group is responsible for that many people

    ● Stress the variety of skills and specialities in the group (span of job titles)

Job Titles

(First) Name	Official Job Title	Number of Direct Reports
	TOTAL	

ICEBREAKERS & ENERGIZERS
3 OF A KIND
A. ASTRO ICEBREAKER (6-12 participants)

LOW

1. Illustrated on the following pages are 12 Astro Icebreaker cards. Print off four copies of each card on to coloured paper. On the CD the cards are grouped in fours for printing on to A4 paper so you will need to cut them out.

2. Select as many identical four card star sign sets as there are participants. Shuffle the selected cards thoroughly. Deal the shuffled cards into new sets of four making sure that no set contains more than one card of the same star sign. Distribute one set to each participant.

3. Since the aim of this inclusion activity is for each participant to interact with as many others as possible, try to ensure that neighbouring participants have no common signs.

4. Explain the rules: the objective is to collect a **complete set of any one star sign** by **exchanging** cards with other participants (like in 'Happy Families'). Only **one** transaction at a time may be made with any participant. For every card given, one must be taken. At no time may any participant have more or less than four cards.

5. As soon as a participant has a complete set, s/he must sit down. Award a prize to the **last** one to sit down, to reward generosity and help to others!

Cancer

Cancer

Gemini

Gemini

Aquarius

Aquarius

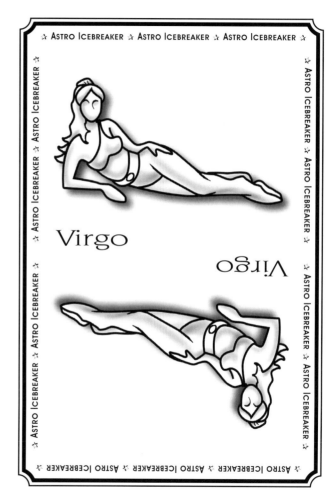

Virgo

Virgo

✣ ASTRO ICEBREAKER ✣
✣ ASTRO ICEBREAKER ✣
✣ ASTRO ICEBREAKER ✣
✣ ASTRO ICEBREAKER ✣
✣ ASTRO ICEBREAKER ✣
✣ ASTRO ICEBREAKER ✣
✣ ASTRO ICEBREAKER ✣

Capricorn

Capricorn

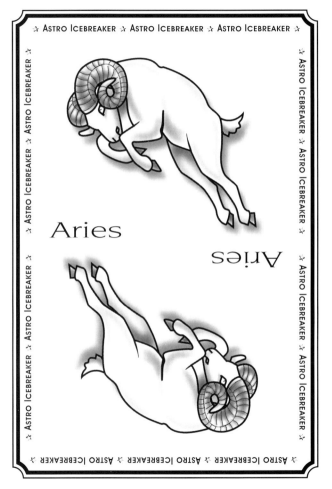

✣ ASTRO ICEBREAKER ✣
✣ ASTRO ICEBREAKER ✣
✣ ASTRO ICEBREAKER ✣
✣ ASTRO ICEBREAKER ✣
✣ ASTRO ICEBREAKER ✣
✣ ASTRO ICEBREAKER ✣
✣ ASTRO ICEBREAKER ✣

Aries

Aries

Libra

Leo

Pisces

Pisces

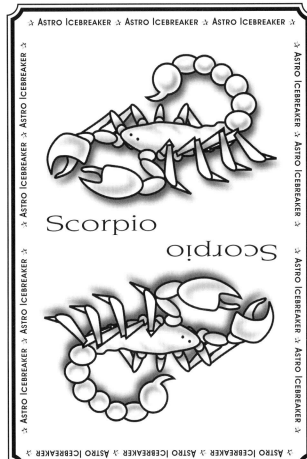

Scorpio

Scorpio

Taurus

Taurus

Sagittarius

Sagittarius

ICEBREAKERS & ENERGIZERS

3 OF A KIND

B. EUROMORN (6-20 participants)

LOW

■ This one has the same design principles as Astro Icebreaker but can be used with up to 20 participants and evokes cultural diversity (a sub-objective?).

1. Illustrated on the following pages are 20 Euromorn cards. Print off four copies of each card on to coloured paper. On the CD the cards are grouped in fours for printing on to A4 paper, so you will need to cut them out.

2. Select as many identical 'good morning' sets as there are participants. Shuffle the selected cards thoroughly. Deal the shuffled cards into new sets of four making sure that no set contains more than one 'good morning' card of the same language. Distribute one set to each participant.

3. Since the aim of this inclusion activity is for each participant to interact with as many others as possible, try to ensure that neighbouring participants have no common language cards.

4. Explain the rules: the objective is to collect a **complete set of one language 'good mornings'** by **exchanging** cards with other participants (like in 'Happy Families'). Only **one** transaction at a time may be made with any participant. For every card given, one must be taken. At no time may any participant have more or less than four cards.

5. As soon as a participant has a complete set of one language, s/he must sit down. Award a prize to the **last** one to sit down, to reward generosity and help to others!

Dobre Jitre!

Dobre Jitre!

Moen!

Moen!

PL

EUROMORN ICEBREAKER EUROMORN ICEBREAKER

PL

EUROMORN ICEBREAKER EUROMORN ICEBREAKER EUROMORN ICEBREAKER

EUROMORN ICEBREAKER EUROMORN ICEBREAKER EUROMORN ICEBREAKER

Dzien Dobry!

Dzien Dobry!

PL PL

EUROMORN ICEBREAKER EUROMORN ICEBREAKER

NL

EUROMORN ICEBREAKER EUROMORN ICEBREAKER

NL

EUROMORN ICEBREAKER EUROMORN ICEBREAKER EUROMORN ICEBREAKER

EUROMORN ICEBREAKER EUROMORN ICEBREAKER EUROMORN ICEBREAKER

Goede Morgen!

Goede Morgen!

NL NL

EUROMORN ICEBREAKER EUROMORN ICEBREAKER

Euromorn Icebreaker   Euromorn Icebreaker   Euromorn Icebreaker

Euromorn Icebreaker   Euromorn Icebreaker   Euromorn Icebreaker

Gruezi!

Good Day!

EUROMORN ICEBREAKER

EUROMORN ICEBREAKER

EUROMORN ICEBREAKER

EUROMORN ICEBREAKER

EUROMORN ICEBREAKER

EUROMORN ICEBREAKER

Morn!

Bonjour!

EUROMORN ICEBREAKER

EUROMORN ICEBREAKER

EUROMORN ICEBREAKER

EUROMORN ICEBREAKER

EUROMORN ICEBREAKER

EUROMORN ICEBREAKER

EUROMORN ICEBREAKER
EUROMORN ICEBREAKER
EUROMORN ICEBREAKER

Bom Dia!
Bom Dia!

EUROMORN ICEBREAKER
EUROMORN ICEBREAKER
EUROMORN ICEBREAKER

EUROMORN ICEBREAKER
EUROMORN ICEBREAKER
EUROMORN ICEBREAKER

Kalimera!
Kalimera!

EUROMORN ICEBREAKER
EUROMORN ICEBREAKER
EUROMORN ICEBREAKER

D EUROMORN ICEBREAKER EUROMORN ICEBREAKER D

Guten Tag!

Guten Tag!

EUROMORN ICEBREAKER EUROMORN ICEBREAKER EUROMORN ICEBREAKER

EUROMORN ICEBREAKER EUROMORN ICEBREAKER EUROMORN ICEBREAKER

D EUROMORN ICEBREAKER EUROMORN ICEBREAKER D

I EUROMORN ICEBREAKER EUROMORN ICEBREAKER I

Bon Giorno!

Bon Giorno!

EUROMORN ICEBREAKER EUROMORN ICEBREAKER EUROMORN ICEBREAKER

EUROMORN ICEBREAKER EUROMORN ICEBREAKER EUROMORN ICEBREAKER

I EUROMORN ICEBREAKER EUROMORN ICEBREAKER I

Grüss Got!

Grüss Got!

God Morgon!

God Morgon!

H

EUROMORN ICEBREAKER EUROMORN ICEBREAKER

H

EUROMORN ICEBREAKER EUROMORN ICEBREAKER EUROMORN ICEBREAKER

Jo Napot!

Jo Napot!

EUROMORN ICEBREAKER EUROMORN ICEBREAKER EUROMORN ICEBREAKER

H

EUROMORN ICEBREAKER EUROMORN ICEBREAKER

H

E

EUROMORN ICEBREAKER EUROMORN ICEBREAKER

E

EUROMORN ICEBREAKER EUROMORN ICEBREAKER EUROMORN ICEBREAKER

Buenas Dias!

Buenas Dias!

EUROMORN ICEBREAKER EUROMORN ICEBREAKER EUROMORN ICEBREAKER

E

EUROMORN ICEBREAKER EUROMORN ICEBREAKER

E

Maidin Mhaith Libh!

Maidin Mhaith Libh!

Bunà Dimineata!

Bunà Dimineata!

DK panel

DK | EUROMORN ICEBREAKER EUROMORN ICEBREAKER | DK

EUROMORN ICEBREAKER

EUROMORN ICEBREAKER

EUROMORN ICEBREAKER

God Morgen!

EUROMORN ICEBREAKER

EUROMORN ICEBREAKER

EUROMORN ICEBREAKER

DK | EUROMORN ICEBREAKER EUROMORN ICEBREAKER | DK

RUS panel

RUS | EUROMORN ICEBREAKER EUROMORN ICEBREAKER | RUS

EUROMORN ICEBREAKER

EUROMORN ICEBREAKER

EUROMORN ICEBREAKER

Dobroe Utro!

EUROMORN ICEBREAKER

EUROMORN ICEBREAKER

EUROMORN ICEBREAKER

RUS | EUROMORN ICEBREAKER EUROMORN ICEBREAKER | RUS

ICEBREAKERS & ENERGIZERS

3 OF A KIND

C. THE 'ICEBREAKER' ICEBREAKER (6-30 participants)

LOW

- ■ The same principle as the previous two but with a 'puzzle-like' objective. Also, it's a 'meta' icebreaker!

1. Print on to white paper as many copies of the 'Icebreaker' picture shown overleaf as you will have participants. Then colour each ship with a different colour. You can do this by hand or, before printing, on your PC (full instructions on the CD).

2. Select as many 'same colour' ships as there are participants. Shuffle the pack thoroughly. Deal the shuffled cards into new sets of four making sure that no set contains more than one icebreaker part of the same colour. (More than one card of the same part is OK as long as the colour is different!) Distribute one card set to each participant.

3. Since the aim of this inclusion activity is for each participant to interact with as many others as possible, try to ensure that neighbouring participants have totally different cards.

4. Explain the rules: the objective is to collect a **complete 'one colour' Icebreaker** by **exchanging** cards with other participants (like in 'Happy Families'). Only **one** transaction may be made with any participant before moving on. For every card given, one must be taken. No participant may have more or less than four cards at any time.

5. As soon as a participant has a complete set, s/he must sit down. Award a prize to the **last** one to complete their 'icebreaker'.

The ICEBREAKER!

ICEBREAKERS & ENERGIZERS

WHOSE SHOES?

HIGH

■ Here's a silly but fun energizer for after lunch on day two or three of a longer course. A similar exercise was invented and conducted with great success on one of our 'Transforming the Trainer' seminars.

■ **Material needed**

- 1 identical paper/plastic bag per participant
- 1 large cardboard box
- 1 numbered A6 card per participant
- 1 score card (overleaf) per participant, printed from the accompanying CD

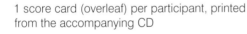

Hmmm

WHOSE SHOES?

1. Ask each participant to remove his/her shoes **under the table** and place them in a bag. Place each bag in the cardboard box and 'mix' them as you collect them.

2. Give the score cards to a participant and ask him/her to distribute them.
    This will distract everyone while you .....

3. Place the pairs of shoes at random (and each with a numbered card) on a table
    either in a nearby group room or in a relatively secluded corner of the main room.

4. Invite participants to visit the 'Whose shoes?' exhibition and note down the
    owners' names on their score card.

5. Award a 'creative' prize to the winner (a clothes peg for the
    nose? some cheese?!)

Tip In courses where communication skills are covered in any way, this energizer brings a powerful message about perception, power of observation and even prejudices.

WHOSE SHOES?

In a moment you will be asked to identify your fellow participants' shoes. Whose shoes correspond with the number next to them?

#	
1	
2	
3	
4	
5	
6	
7	
8	
9	
10	
11	
12	
13	
14	
15	
16	
17	
18	
19	
20	

ICEBREAKERS & ENERGIZERS

HEXASLOGANS

LOW

- Fun, fast moving and relevant to course coverage!

1. Select a slogan which represents one of the training messages you wish to get across during the course, and which has roughly the same number of letters as the number of participants – or twice as many (Examples: 'Winning for Customers', 'Communicate', 'Safety First!' etc, etc.)

2. From the CD print an appropriate number of hexagons and write one letter of the slogan on each. Give one or two to each participant. (If there are too many participants, give blanks, speech marks or exclamation marks!)

3. Stick three or four flip chart sheets side by side on a wall or whiteboard and spray with non-permanent spray glue (if you don't have pinboards or Post-its*).

4. Ask **all** the participants to come and together try to arrange their letters into the correct sequence in record time (time them so that there **is** a record to beat on the next course!). The hexagons fit together elegantly and require more jostling than normal Post-its, ie: more icebreaking!

Note *Ready-made hexagons are available from Neuland dealers throughout Europe. In the UK: Pinpoint Facilitation, 10 Monument Park, Warpsgrove Lane, Chalgrove, Oxfordshire OX44 7RW. Tel: 01865 400777 Fax: 01865 400666 Email: makethedifference@pinpoint-facilitation.com Web: www.pinpoint-facilitation.com*

*For Post-it hexagons contact VIS-IT: Vision Works, 10755 East Tamarisk Way, Scottsdale, AZ 85262 USA. Tel: 888 439 7237 Fax: 480 595 1816 Web: www.vis-it.com

ICEBREAKERS & ENERGIZERS

TELL-TALE OBJECTS

MEDIUM

- A 'serious' inclusion activity especially suited to behavioural courses. It invites medium to high self-disclosure.

1. Select a number of small, evocative and unusual objects (eg: a piece of quartz, a wooden egg, a souvenir Eiffel Tower, a yo-yo, etc) and place them on a tray at the entrance to the training room (50% more objects than participants).

2. Ask each participant, as they enter the room, to choose an object and take it to their place.

3. The icebreaker consists simply of asking each person (in turn or at random) to introduce themselves and say **why** they chose that particular object. People usually find plenty of self-revealing things to say but, if anyone clams up, don't push them. As always, silence speaks louder than words!

MAMA!

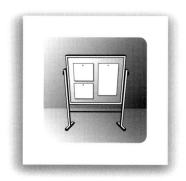

UNIVERSAL
EXERCISE DESIGNS

UNIVERSAL EXERCISE DESIGNS
JIGSAW LEARNING

■ A seemingly complex but devastatingly powerful way of ensuring that learning takes place. Particularly applicable to technical courses.

1. Choose three 'chunks' of an overall training message you need to get across, and which can be learned in approximately 15 minutes.

2. Split the class into three groups and expose each group to one of the learning chunks.

Eg: ● One group learns from a checklist a step-by-step procedure for completing the XYZ process correctly; they check their understanding with each other

● The second group learns from the trainer the actual skills needed for, say, step 5; they practise or role play to ensure they can do it

● The third group reads an article on the legal implications of incorrectly carrying out the procedure, and they discuss examples, etc, with one another to ensure understanding

3. **Regroup** into new teams (see table overleaf) where at least one participant from each of the original groups now **teaches** the others what they learned.

Note *It's called Jigsaw Learning because each participant takes a piece of the puzzle into the second groupings. When we have to **teach** others, that's when we really learn!*

UNIVERSAL EXERCISE DESIGNS

JIGSAW LEARNING

- Choose three separate elements to be learned
- Divide total group into **vertical** teams and give a number to each member following chart; expose each team to a different element (15 minutes' teaching or study)
- Now create new teams by numbers (all 1's, all 2's, etc); ask each member to teach all the members of the new group what they have learned

3 SUBJECTS (TOTAL PARTICIPANTS 16)	3 SUBJECTS (17)	3 SUBJECTS (18)	3 SUBJECTS (19)	3 SUBJECTS (20)
1 2 3 4 5	1 2 3 4 5	1 2 3 4 5 6	1 2 3 4 5 6	1 2 3 4 5 6
1 2 3 4 5	1 2 3 4 5 5	1 2 3 4 5 6	1 2 3 4 5 6	1 2 3 4 5 6 6
1 2 3 4 5 5	1 2 3 4 5 5	1 2 3 4 5 6	1 2 3 4 5 6 6	1 2 3 4 5 6 6
TOTAL PARTICIPANTS 16	**17**	**18**	**19**	**20**

3 SUBJECTS (6)	(7)	(8)	(9)	(10)	(11)	(12)	(13)	(14)	(15)
1 2	1 2	1 2	1 2 3	1 2 3	1 2 3	1 2 3 4	1 2 3 4	1 2 3 4	1 2 3 4 5
1 2	1 2	1 2 2	1 2 3	1 2 3	1 2 3 3	1 2 3 4	1 2 3 4	1 2 3 4 4	1 2 3 4 5
1 2	1 2 2	1 2 2	1 2 3	1 2 3 3	1 2 3 3	1 2 3 4	1 2 3 4 4	1 2 3 4 4	1 2 3 4 5
TOTAL PARTICIPANTS 6	**7**	**8**	**9**	**10**	**11**	**12**	**13**	**14**	**15**

UNIVERSAL EXERCISE DESIGNS
MUSICAL WALLS

■ This is a 'high energy' exercise design adaptable to just about **any** training context with 10–12 participants.

1. Prepare three double-sided white or pin boards (or six flip charts) with a brainstorming type question, which you'd like participants to answer, written on each side.

   Examples:
   - How could we improve our meetings?
   - Can you find three ways to speed up bureaucracy?
   - What to do to improve communication?
   - How could we increase motivation?
   - How to instill more team spirit?

2. Divide each board into five or six sections (number them but don't always have the same numbered section on the same part of the board, otherwise some pairs will always be stretching or always on their knees!).

3. Divide the group into pairs (pair 1, 2, 3, 4, 5, 6) plus one or two singles depending on total number.

4. Station each pair in front of a 'question' board and tell them to keep writing brainstorm answers to the question in 'their' space until the music stops.

5. Play music for 4–5 minutes then stop and move every pair round clockwise to next board.

6. Continue till all have worked on each question.

7. Note/photograph each board. Discuss and/or issue a copy to each participant.

UNIVERSAL EXERCISE DESIGNS

FORCE FIELD ANALYSIS

1. DEFINITION

Force Field Analysis is a device for understanding problem situations and planning corrective actions. As such, it is applicable in many training/facilitation contexts where real-life issues are being discussed. The FFA technique views any problem situation as being an equilibrium – the result of the operation of various opposing forces. Moving to a more desirable state of affairs (desired situation) can only be achieved by upsetting the equilibrium, moving it and stabilising it in the new position.

To move the equilibrium, you must alter the forces – add more driving forces or reduce the restraining ones.

UNIVERSAL EXERCISE DESIGNS

FORCE FIELD ANALYSIS

2. THE STEPS

1. Choose the problem situation you wish to work on. Describe it carefully. What is the **present** state? Write an abbreviated version in the centre of a board.

2. Carefully describe the desired situation. What would you like things to look like? Write an abbreviated version to the right of the present state.

3. Identify the forces operating in your force field. List the forces which are pushing towards the desired situation (left) and those pushing away from it (right). (You might get participants to write forces on Post-its and stick them on the board.)

4. Examine the forces and apply a weighting to each of them (group consensus).

5. Consider the strategies for moving the equilibrium. In other words:
   ● Add more driving forces (difficult)
   ● Reduce restraining forces (easier)
   Select several important restraining forces and brainstorm plans to reduce them. Propose some new driving forces and discuss implementation plans.

6. Implement the action plans.

7. Plan how to stabilise the force field once the desired state has been reached.

FORCE FIELD ANALYSIS
3. EXAMPLE

- Thanks to Paul Donovan for supplying the information on FFA.

UNIVERSAL EXERCISE DESIGNS
DETECTIVE ENQUIRY

- A kind of learning 'Cluedo' for individuals, pairs or teams. Useful as a recap device or at any time to add interest to dull subjects.

1. Think up a mystery question concerning the course subject matter.

   Example from a Train-the-Trainer Course:

   'What is Sherlock Trainer's **TASK**?

   Answer:

   To teach **T**echniques, help change **A**ttitudes, train to improve **S**kills and provide **K**nowledge.

2. Create a series of clues which lead participants progressively to the answer. They could be hidden handouts, words or phrases from books or articles, anagrams or crossword-type clues, etc.

3. Award a prize for the first individual, pair or team to find the answer to the mystery question.

UNIVERSAL EXERCISE DESIGNS
ROLE DEBATE

- An action-oriented 'case-study' way of helping participants confront new ideas and methods. It's useful at any time to replace a traditional case study whenever you need to challenge the status quo and help people see both sides of the picture.

1. Write or find a very short article/statement/report which takes a strong position for or against a new way of doing things. Give a copy to each participant.

   Example: A paragraph from a report advocating a company-wide change from MAC to PC.

2. When they've read it, divide participants into groups of four and allocate roles of:
   - Facilitator – to be a discussion leader without opinion
   - Supporter – to be very much in favour of the report
   - Devil's Advocate – to argue strenuously **against** the report
   - Consultant – to be coldly factual and boringly statistical!

   Tip You may want to give people whose opinions you know the **opposite** role to play!

3. Allow 10–20 minutes for the discussion and ask each participant to adopt the role fully, even if (especially if!) it's not their real opinion.

4. Ask the facilitators to report conclusions. Discuss why roles were difficult/easy and what was learned by changing role.

UNIVERSAL EXERCISE DESIGNS
DIVIDING PARTICIPANTS INTO SMALL GROUPS
1. PARTICIPANT-LED SELECTION

A. Ask participants to vote on whether groups should be set up according to similarity or complementarity.

B. Brainstorm 5–10 criteria which represent similarity or complementarity.

C. Give participants self-adhesive dots or pens and allow them three votes to distribute to their preferred criteria.

D. Short-list top three criteria.

E. Give participants paper badges on which to write their names. Ask them to form groups by sticking badges on the board, ensuring that each group's composition matches the criteria chosen.
This may mean some jockeying and changing (that's part of the process) until the groups are balanced. The big advantage of this methodology is that nobody feels they have been set up.

UNIVERSAL EXERCISE DESIGNS

DIVIDING PARTICIPANTS INTO SMALL GROUPS

2. DARTS

A. Cut out a paper cover for a normal dartboard and divide into 'group' sections.

B. Give each participant a dart and ask them to aim at one of the sections and throw the dart when they're ready. Ask them to remember which group they select.

C. Once one group section is complete, only accept throws which land in another section (otherwise, throw again).

Note *Obviously, one or two of the participants are left with little choice. The method is relatively random anyway, except that it favours good darts players who can also remember whose dart went where so that they can aim to join the same or another group. So .....?!*

UNIVERSAL EXERCISE DESIGNS

NOTES

7 WONDERS
CONSENSUS-SEEKING

SEVEN WONDERS
DESCRIPTIONS & OBJECTIVES

Trainers tell me that they are constantly on the look-out for new exercises which help teams with the emotionally difficult problem of group decision-making through consensus-seeking.

Seven Wonders is a deceptively simple exercise which gets right to the heart of the problem. How can teams reach a consensus when each member 'owns' an opinion (or a part of the resources) which he or she is unwilling to give up? It's been shown that it is relatively difficult to get too emotionally involved when one is asked to select items for survival on the moon or in a shipwrecked raft. But here it's different.

The team's task is first to select, **as individuals**, the seven most wondrous, awe-inspiring 'things' which they think should replace the all-but-disappeared ancient wonders of the world. That's the easy part.

Next, they must join a 5–8 person group and are given 30 minutes to reach a consensus on the **group's** choice for the new Seven Wonders.

Obviously, the learning comes from how they decide to decide, and the process of give and take, compromise, logical argument versus emotion, etc, gives every trainer ample scope for discussion and message-building.

SEVEN WONDERS
TRAINER'S GUIDE

To help teams practise group decision-making through consensus-seeking. To simulate the difficulties involved in compromising on personal values/opinions in the interests of group performance.

To give group leaders the opportunity to practise consensus-building with a (relatively) harmless decision.

To practise facilitation skills.

60 minutes

1. Prepare yourself for the exercise by working through each step in your mind. Make your **own** decision on the new Seven Wonders.

2. Create an appropriate number of handouts (see page 52).

3. Explain the objectives of the exercise to the target group and distribute one Instructions Card and one Worksheet to each participant.

4. Allow 10 minutes for each participant to establish their personal list – using any criteria they wish.

5. Divide the participants into teams of 5–8 members and appoint leaders (if applicable to your objectives).

6. Locate each team in a separate room and allow them 30 minutes to reach a group consensus and to write their final list on a flip chart.

7. Reconvene and ask each team to present their list.

8. Lead a review discussion following the suggestion on page 53.

SEVEN WONDERS
PREPARATION

From the CD print off one copy of the Team Instructions Card and the Worksheet for each participant.

SEVEN WONDERS
TRAINER'S REVIEW GUIDE & TIPS

Here are some suggested questions for discussion following the teams' presentations, based on several years' experience using Seven Wonders with specialist and management teams from all over the world.

● What was the team's (final) decision-making system? How did they decide to decide? Did they stick to it?

  Note In some groups, consensus is reached on a 'category'-based list (eg: one from science, one from buildings, one from nature, etc), but then a member sways a majority away to another list.

● To what extent did team members become emotionally involved in their choices? How did the others deal with the situation? Ask "How close was this to the reality back on the job?".

  Note Reactions in groups vary from cold indifference ("I didn't care either way about my list or anyone else's") to total ownership ("I felt I had to insist that we include the telephone – I mean it's revolutionised everything in the world!"). Some people are jubilant, some sulk, others try to trade and manipulate to get their own way.

● What could/should the team leader and the members have done differently to achieve more harmony and consensus in the team?

TEAM INSTRUCTIONS CARD

All seven of the ancient wonders of the world, except the pyramids, have disappeared*. So why shouldn't we invent some new ones?! In a BBC television programme, seven famous scientists were asked to do just that. Their choices ranged from space travel and the flight of the albatross, to the retina of the eye and the garden snail! But you don't have to have a Nobel Prize to do this exercise which is divided into two parts.

1 *Your Selection*

*Working individually, please come up with **your** seven wonders. Which do you think are the seven most amazing things in the world? Which things (past or present, simple or complex, large or small) always fill you with awe every time you think about them? Don't restrict yourself to buildings like in the ancient list. Think about technical inventions, nature, geography, the arts, construction ... anything! The only limit is your imagination. Please use the Worksheet for your notes and final selection. You have 10 minutes to choose your Seven Wonders.*

2 *Group Selection*

*The next step will be an exercise in consensus decision-making. Working as a team, the task will be to produce an agreed **group** selection. This agreement may not be easy to reach but try to make sure that each member is willing to accept each decision as you proceed. Record your team's final list on the Worksheet, then write it up on a flip chart sheet ready to present to the class.*

Guidelines
- *The most important thing for the team to decide will be **how** to decide!*
- *Listen to **everybody's** opinion*
- *Don't argue too long for your own ideas, but don't give up too easily either*

3 *Score*

Give yourself one point for every one of your Seven Wonders which ends up in the team's final selection.

* They were: the Lighthouse at Alexandria, the Colossus of Rhodes, the Hanging Gardens of Babylon, Artemis' temple at Ephesus, the Mausoleum at Halicarnassus, the Pyramids and the Statue of Zeus at Olympia.

7 WONDERS

WORKSHEET

YOUR SELECTION

- _____
- _____
- _____
- _____
- _____
- _____
- _____

SCORE

GROUP SELECTION

- _____
- _____
- _____
- _____
- _____
- _____
- _____

7 WONDERS

SEVEN WONDERS

NOTES

TERRA NOVA
LEADERSHIP & PLANNING

TERRA NOVA

DESCRIPTION & OBJECTIVES

Terra Nova was designed as a team planning exercise to help groups learn how to process complex information and choose logically between a number of alternatives.

There is no right answer (apart from making correct calculations of the cost of each alternative) and this makes it an ideal simulation for leadership seminars. As John Kotter of Harvard Business School has reported, one of the key characteristics of successful leaders is their ability to 'set direction' and let the managers and the team get on with the planning. In this exercise, the group's decision depends on the strategy they adopt.

Terra Nova is a fictitious area of Newfoundland and the team has been dropped by float plane on Pine Lake. Their task is to reach **any one** of the five lakes on an adjacent island so as to be picked up again by the plane. There is at least one alternative way of getting to each of the lakes (bus, ferries, hiking, 4-wheel drive hire, plane, rafting, etc), some faster and more expensive than others. They are asked to cost at least three alternative methods/routes and tell the pilot where to pick them up before he takes off. Their decision will obviously depend on whether they (or the leader) decide on speed, cost, adventure, physical activity, etc, as the strategy to adopt.

TERRA NOVA
TRAINER'S GUIDE

To give participants the opportunity to practise leadership skills. To allow teams of 4–9 members to practise planning, organising data and decision-making.

To demonstrate the need for co-operation, sharing and synergy in a team, especially during the planning of a project.

± 90 minutes

1. Familiarise yourself with the Team Instructions Card, the Terra Nova map and the 15 information cards. Go through the suggestions (page 60) and make sure you understand them. Make up an appropriate number of card sets (page 61).

2. Divide the participants into teams of 4–9 members and explain the objectives of the Terra Nova exercise.

3. Distribute a Team Instructions Card, a map and $500 (card) to each member of each team.

4. While they are reading the instructions, shuffle and distribute to each member of each team their share of the 15 information cards.

5. Allow five minutes for assimilation/questions, etc.

6. Set the stop watch for one hour.

7. Reconvene and ask each team to report on their decided route and costing/rationale.

8. Go through the review questions on page 62 with each team.

TERRA NOVA

SUGGESTED OPTIONS, TIMING & COSTINGS
(Based on 25 control groups' solutions)

OPTION/ROUTE	TIMING	COST per person	(Team of 6)
HIKING A. 1. Walk to Crossroads 2. Bus to St Paul 3. Buy food 4. Hovercraft to Walkabout Point 5. Hike to Moose Lake via Elk and Moose Refuges & camping	June 21st: St Paul 22nd: Moose Trail (camp) 23rd: Elk Refuge 24th: Moose Refuge 25th: Moose Trail (camp) 26th: Moose Lake (pm) pick up	Bus = $10 Hovercraft = $150 Refuges = $30 Food = +/- $100	$290 (+ Hotel, St Paul?)
HIKING B. 1. Walk to Crossroads 2. Bus to Seal Bay 3. Ferry to Deer Point 4. Hike to Deer Lake	June 21st: Seal Bay 27th: Deer Point – Vinland Bay 28th: Deer Lake (late) 29th: Deer Lake (am) pick up	Bus = $50 Ferry = $150 Food = +/- $100	$300 (+ Hotel, Seal Bay?)
LAND ROVER 1. Walk to Crossroads 2. Bus to St Paul 3. Land Rover to Seal Bay 4. Ferry to Longship Landing 5. Track to St Brendan 6. Hike to Monk's Lake	June 21st: Seal Bay 23rd: Longship Landing to 'Ford' 24th: St Brendan 25th: Monk's Lake (pm) pick up	Bus = $10 Ferry = $108 *($50 + $350÷6)* Food = $100 Car Hire = $75 *(3 days hire* *$450÷6)*	$293 (+ Hotels, Seal Bay, St Brendan?)
RAFTING 1. Walk to Crossroads 2. Bus to St Peter 3. Ferry to Serpent Point 4. Hike to Serpent Source 5. Raft to Vinland Bay 6. Hike to Deer Lake	June 21st: St Peter 22nd: Serpent Source 23rd–25th: River – Vinland Bay 26th: Deer Lake (pm) pick up	Bus = $10 Ferry = $50 Raft = $160 *(+$600 ÷ 6 = $100 deposit)* Food = $100	$320 (+ Hotel, St Peter?)
PLANE 1. Walk to Crossroads 2. Bus to Prince Anthony 3. Plane to Fisherman's Island 4. Ferry to St Patrick's Bay 5. Hike to Viking Lake	June 21st: Prince Anthony (stay till 25th) 25th: Fisherman's Island 26th: St Patrick's Bay – Viking Lake (arrive pm) pick up	Bus = $18 Plane = $350 Ferry = $50 Food = $82 (!)	$500 (No money left for hotels!)

TERRA NOVA
PREPARATION

1. From the CD print off one copy of the Map, Team Instructions Card and $500 card for each participant in each of the teams.

2. Now print off from the CD one set of the 15 Information Cards for each team, changing the colour of the paper for each set. One set to be divided equally between the members of one team.

TERRA NOVA

TRAINER REVIEW GUIDE

During the exercise make sure you spend time with each group to observe the way in which they get themselves organised and, above all, how the leader guides them towards making a sound and rational choice which satisfies everyone in the team. Things to look and listen for:

- Does the leader 'set direction' at the beginning by discussing a **strategic** approach to the problem? In other words, does s/he talk through whether the team should go for speed, economy, adventure or whatever **before** jumping into the specific details involved in calculating options?

- Does the leader help the team organise itself by considering one option at a time rather than moving from one problem to another as the cards are read out?

- To what extent do team members share information and co-operate with each other?

- How good a job does the team do in planning the **details** of each alternative route (timing/costing, etc)? Do they consider where to spend the night, either camping or spending money on hotels? The amount of detail in their plan is an interesting pointer to their whole planning process.

- During the review session, ask each group to comment on the **way** in which they came to their decision (process) and give your own feedback.

TERRA NOVA
TIPS FOR TRAINERS

Here are some tips arising from the experience of running Terra Nova with 25 control groups from a number of multi-national companies:

- Leaders often fail to 'set direction' and get bogged down with the planning of each of the options. This means that, by the time the team gets to choose between walking, rafting, driving, etc, arguments arise between those who prefer one option or the other. If leaders first set direction ('We'll go for the fastest/cheapest/most adventurous solution'), then decision-making is much easier and motivation higher.

- Don't jump in immediately if a team fails to notice that certain ferries don't take vehicles – they'll realise soon enough and the learning is deeper if they make this kind of mistake.

- Teams often over/under estimate how far a healthy 35–50 year old can walk in a day. Consensus now seems to say that 40 kilometres would be reasonable in this situation – but it's **their** feet!

- Always accept the teams' judgement of timing (unless they make calculation mistakes). It's **their** exercise!

TEAM INSTRUCTIONS CARD

Imagine that you and your team are in the second week of a one month management course in Newfoundland, Canada. The 'Planning' part of the course is to be conducted as an outdoor, teambuilding exercise. The group left Gander International Airport this morning at dawn and were flown north in a small float plane to the (fictitious) area shown on the map.

1 *It is now 07.30 hours and today is Wednesday, June 21st.*

*You have just landed on **Pine Lake** (middle, right side of map) which is about 60 kilometres south of Prince Anthony – the biggest town in the area.*

*The pilot will take off again in about 45 minutes and has given **each** of you two envelopes. One contains the information cards you have in front of you and the other contains $500 in cash. In addition, you are each carrying a back pack with a small tent, a sleeping bag, a two litre water bottle and a change of underclothes. You are dressed in heavy-duty, all-weather clothes (anorak, waterproof trousers and sturdy boots). You have no other money or equipment. The pilot has told you that he will pick you up on **any one of the lakes on Brendan Island** but that he is not authorised to land on the sea.*

2 *The group's task right now is to plan your journey so you can tell the pilot where and when to pick you up and fly you back to Gander. As you plan the trip, here are the questions you should answer:*

OBJECTIVE? ● *Which of the possible destinations will you choose?*

DEADLINE? ● *How long will it take you to get there?*

ACTION? ● *Which of the alternative routes will you choose (please mark the route and overnight stops on the map)*

● *What different methods of transport will you use?*

● *How much will it cost you?*
(Please evaluate and cost at least three alternatives)

To answer these questions, you have 60 minutes and will need all the information on the cards plus, of course, the map.
Please READ your information cards to the others when you feel it will be useful to the group (or when asked to do so by the leader).
Please don't write on any of the information cards, only on the map.
The group will be judged on its rational use of time, money and the human resources of its members.

Good luck!

TERRA NOVA

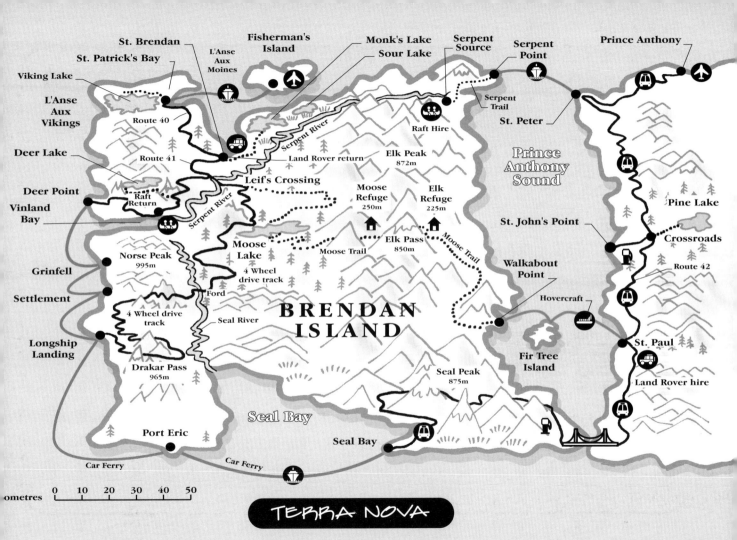

Viking Lake
St. Brendan
St. Patrick's Bay
L'Anse Aux Moines
Fisherman's Island
Monk's Lake
Sour Lake
Serpent Source
Serpent Point
Prince Anthony

L'Anse Aux Vikings

Route 40

Deer Lake

Route 41

Serpent River

Serpent Trail
St. Peter

Deer Point
Vinland Bay

Raft Return

Leif's Crossing

Land Rover return

Elk Peak
872m

Prince Anthony Sound

Serpent River

Moose Refuge
250m

Elk Refuge
225m

Pine Lake

St. John's Point

Crossroads

Grinfell

Norse Peak
995m

Moose Lake

4 Wheel drive track

Moose Trail

Elk Pass
850m

Moose Trail

Route 42

Settlement

Ford

Walkabout Point

Longship Landing

4 Wheel drive track

Seal River

BRENDAN ISLAND

Hovercraft

St. Paul

Land Rover hire

Drakar Pass
965m

Fir Tree Island

Seal Peak
875m

Port Eric

Seal Bay

Seal Bay

Car Ferry

Car Ferry

ometres   0   10   20   30   40   50

TERRA NOVA

OBJECTIVE

The pilot will pick you up on **any one** of the lakes on Brendan Island (just tell him which one ... and when) but is not authorised to land on the sea

TERRA NOVA

The Elk Pass and Moose Refuge Chalets charge
$15 per person per night

The Moose Trail hiking track from Walkabout Point to Moose Lake
is 155 kilometres long and passes through
breathtaking scenery

4

There are shops, a hotel and a gas station in these towns:

- **Prince Anthony**
- **St. Peter**
- **St. Paul**
- **Seal Bay**
- **Longship Landing**
- **St. Brendan**

The sea plane charter company will charge a penalty
of $50 per hour of waiting if you are not
at the designated lake on time

*The track from Longship Landing
to Leif's Crossing (one of the most spectacular in
Newfoundland) is 195 kilometres long and is only suitable
for 4-wheel drive, diesel vehicles
(rough terrain, mountain passes and river fords)*

7

FOR HIRE

Diesel, Seats 8, Full Gas Tanks 2 x 50 litres
(20 litres per 100km. $1 per litre)

HIRE AND RETURN

• **ST. PAUL**   • **ST. BRENDAN**

$150
PER DAY

• UNLIMITED KILOMETRES •

Note No other rental facilities are available.

TERRA NOVA

ROAD DISTANCES

Prince Anthony to Seal Bay (in kilometres)	PRINCE ANTHONY	ST. PETER	CROSSROADS	ST. PAUL	SEAL BAY
PRINCE ANTHONY	–	48	165	233	432
ST. PETER	48	–	117	215	384
CROSSROADS	165	117	–	68	267
ST. PAUL	233	215	68	–	199
SEAL BAY	432	384	267	199	–

PRINCE ANTHONY SOUND
PASSENGER FERRY

DAILY SERVICE

ST. PETER –
SERPENT POINT

$50 *per person each way*

ST. PETER	SERPENT POINT	SERPENT POINT	ST. PETER
09.00	**12.30**	**14.00**	**17.00**

FIR TREE ISLAND HOVERCRAFT

DAILY SERVICE

Sorry – No Vehicles

ST. PAUL – FIR TREE ISLAND – WALKABOUT POINT

$150 *per person each way*

ST. PAUL	FIR TREE ISLAND	WALKABOUT POINT	WALKABOUT POINT	FIR TREE ISLAND	ST. PAUL
09.00	09.30	10.00	11.15	11.45	12.15
13.30	14.00	14.30	15.45	16.15	16.45

NEWFOUNDLAND LEVRIER

DAILY SERVICE

PRINCE ANTHONY – SEAL BAY

PRINCE ANTHONY TO SEAL BAY	
PRINCE ANTHONY	08.30
— $8 —	
ST. PETER	09.30
— $10 —	
CROSSROADS	12.00
— $10 —	
ST. PAUL	13.00
— $40 —	
SEAL BAY	17.00

SEAL BAY TO PRINCE ANTHONY	
SEAL BAY	06.00
— $40 —	
ST. PAUL	10.00
— $10 —	
CROSSROADS	11.00
— $10 —	
ST. PETER	13.30
— $8 —	
PRINCE ANTHONY	14.30

TERRA NOVA

Brend*air*

SUNDAY SERVICE ONLY

Prince Anthony –
Fisherman's Island – Prince Anthony

$350
*per person
each way*

Prince Anthony	Fisherman's Island	Fisherman's Island	Prince Anthony
15.00	**15.30**	**16.00**	**16.30**

FISHERMAN'S ISLAND FERRIES INC.

Monday to Friday only

$50 *per person each way*

FISHERMAN'S ISLAND – ST. PATRICK'S BAY

Fisherman's Island	St. Patrick's Bay	St. Patrick's Bay	Fisherman's Island
08.00	**12.00**	**13.00**	**17.00**

SEAL BAY – DEER POINT
CAR FERRY

JUNE	ARRIVE		DEPART	
SEAL BAY	———		Thu June 22	**10.00**
PORT ERIC	Thu June 22	**16.00**	Fri June 23	**07.00**
LONGSHIP LANDING	Fri June 23	**15.00**	Mon June 26	**06.00**
SETTLEMENT	Mon June 26	**09.00**	Mon June 26	**12.00**
GRINFELL	Mon June 26	**15.00**	Tue June 27	**08.00**
DEER POINT	Tue June 27	**13.00**	———	

Fares: Seal Bay–Longship Landing = $350 per vehicle + $50 per person
Seal Bay–Deer Point = $450 per vehicle + $150 per person

3 DAYS RAFTING ADVENTURE

$160 per person + $600 refundable deposit

- **Hire a raft (4–9 persons)**
- **Ride the river and the rapids from Serpent Source to Vinland Bay.**

Departure every Friday at 09.00. Arrival in Vinland Bay, Sunday evening.
Please bring tent, sleeping bag and food for the trip.

TERRA NOVA

16

$500

TERRA NOVA

TERRA NOVA

NOTES

VIKING ATTACK!
TEAMBUILDING

VIKING ATTACK!

DESCRIPTION & OBJECTIVES

Viking Attack is a teambuilding exercise which you can use in any number of training situations.

It has proved to be my most useful and consistently popular exercise. Basically, each team is given a set of 33 information cards (most relevant, some 'red herring'), distributed at random among them, and is asked to work against the clock to discover when and where a fictitious Viking Attack took place. In order to simulate the need for **complementarity** and **interdependence** in successful teams, members must not show their cards to each other – only read them.

Although it seems a simple problem to solve, the team must elect a **leader, set an objective, organise** and **delegate** the processing of information and listen to each other, if they want to come close to the present world record of 8 minutes 56 seconds for finding the three-part solution. This was set, perhaps unsurprisingly, by a group of Scandinavian/British Midland airline pilots! However, groups of bankers, company directors and engineers have all succeeded within 15 minutes. The average time taken is 21 minutes 20 seconds and the longest was 1 hour 45 minutes by a group of American company vice-presidents!

VIKING ATTACK!
TRAINER'S GUIDE

To allow groups of 5–7 members to practise teambuilding skills.
To demonstrate the need for leadership in a team.

To show how successful teams need complementary skills (in this case logical thinking, map-reading, calculating ...) and are interdependent.

To underline the vital importance of listening to other team members.

To give teams the opportunity to organise and delegate the processing of information.

World record – 8'56"
World average – 21'20"
Top 10 within 15 minutes

1. Familiarise yourself with the Team Instructions Card and with the 33 clue cards (32 + map). Go through the solution (page 86) using the clue cards as a guide. Make up an appropriate number of card sets (page 87).

2. Divide the participants into groups of 5–7, give each member a Team Instructions Card, and explain the objectives of the exercise (all or any of the objectives suggested in the panel left).

3. Inform the teams of the time scores obtained by other groups (see panel) and allow each team five minutes to elect a leader and set their own time objective and/or fix any other objectives they wish (eg: team spirit, motivational climate in group, etc).

4. During these five minutes take one set of cards per team, shuffle them and distribute evenly to each team member FACE DOWN.

5. Locate teams out of earshot of each other and ask them to turn over the cards and start the problem-solving when you start your stopwatch.

6. As soon as each team gives you their three correct answers (June 30th, 864 A.D., Rouen) note the exact time from your stopwatch.

7. Reconvene when the last team has found the solution and go through the questions on the Trainer Review Guide (page 88).

VIKING ATTACK!
SOLUTION

THE VIKING ATTACK TOOK PLACE ON JUNE 30TH, 864 A.D. AT ROUEN.

R A T I O N A L E

DATE Although Thorskild had arrived by June 26th (11 days from Oslo) and the required 375 warriors by June 28th (13 days from Oslo), they were unarmed and the weapons on Longship Number 13 did not arrive until June 29th. However, because June 15th was a Sunday, June 29th was the fifth Sunday in June. Since Viking superstition prevented violence on that day, the attack took place on June 30th.

YEAR

Thorskild's father became King	= 843
He died 16 years later / Thorskild (36 yrs old) crowned	= 859
Thorskild was 41 on day of attack = 859 + 5	= 864

PLACE Using the rough scale of kilometres on the map + the compass rose, the four first legs took the Vikings to the Seine estuary and the 90° turn to port (left) took them up river (where they saw peasants on either bank) to Rouen.

VIKING ATTACK!
PREPARATION

1. From the CD print off one copy of the Team Instructions Card for each participant.

2. Now print off from the CD one set of the 33 Clue Cards (including the map) for each team, changing the colour of the paper for each set. One set to be divided equally between the members of one team.

VIKING ATTACK!

TRAINER REVIEW GUIDE

During the exercise, make sure you spend time with each team to observe how they go about solving the problem. Things to look for and give feedback on:

- **LEADERSHIP** – Who was the elected/real leader?! What styles were displayed (directive, supportive, delegating, abdicating, etc?)

- **PLANNING** – How was the problem-solving approach planned? Did the team agree on how they would process information? Did they stick to their plan?

- **ORGANISING** – How well did they organise data (eg: arrival of longships, direction of legs, calculation of year, etc)?

- **COMMUNICATING** – How well did the team members listen to each other? How often did an information card have to be repeated? Did the team pick up on **Sunday** June 15th immediately? Did they control their own information-giving in order to tie it in with others' information?

- **INTERDEPENDENCE** – How well did team members build on each other's information and ideas?

TEAM INSTRUCTIONS CARD

Sometime during the Viking era, a fictitious Norse leader sets out with a fleet of longships to plunder a european settlement. Your task is to determine on what date, in which year and where the Viking attack took place.

1 *You may share the information you have on the cards with other members but you may not show your cards to each other.*

2 *When your group has reached the solution, please write your three answers on a sheet of paper and hand it to the Facilitator who will ask you for your rationale.*

Please do not write on any of the cards.

VIKING ATTACK!

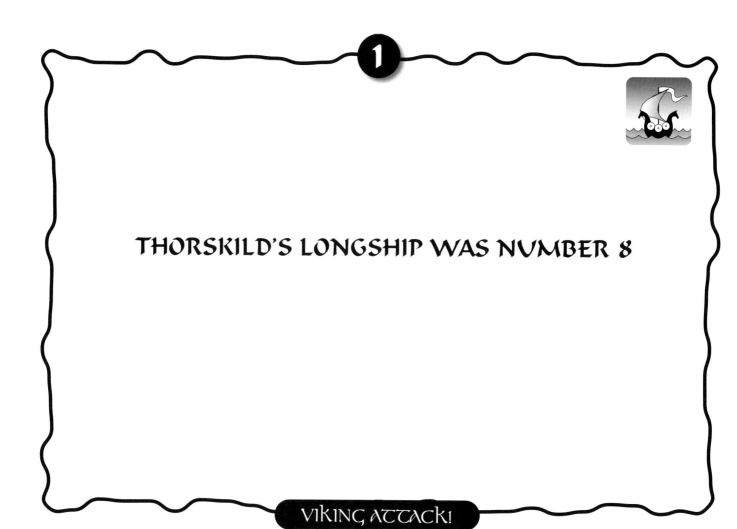

1

THORSKILD'S LONGSHIP WAS NUMBER 8

VIKING ATTACK!

FOR THE PURPOSE OF THIS EXERCISE, IT CAN BE ASSUMED THAT THE CALENDAR DAYS AND MONTHS FOLLOWED EXACTLY THE SAME PATTERN AS THEY DO TODAY

EACH LONGSHIP (EXCEPT NUMBER 13) CARRIED 40 UNARMED VIKING WARRIORS

LONGSHIPS NUMBER 6, 7, 9, 10, 14 AND 15
TOOK 7 DAYS TO REACH THE BATTLE SITE
FROM OSLO

FOR THE LAST LEG OF THE VOYAGE, THE
LONGSHIPS TURNED 90 DEGREES TO THE
PORT SIDE & SOON PEASANTS RIDING IN
WOODEN CHARIOTS WERE SEEN ON BOTH
SIDES OF THE SHIPS

VIKING ATTACK!

NO BATTLE COULD EVER BE FOUGHT WITHOUT
THE VIKING LEADER

THORSKILD WAS THE LEADER OF THE EXPEDITION

LONGSHIPS NUMBER 4 AND 13 ARRIVED AT THE BATTLE SITE 7 DAYS AFTER LONGSHIP NUMBER 6

HARALD AND HIS FOLLOWERS WERE IN
LONGSHIP NUMBER 5. THEY HAD SUCCESSFULLY
CONDUCTED A PREVIOUS ATTACK ON THE
EAST COAST OF IRELAND

ALL THE LONGSHIPS FOLLOWED THE SAME
COURSE FOR THE VOYAGE WHICH WAS
DIVIDED INTO A NUMBER OF LEGS

VIKING ATTACK!

FOR THE SECOND LEG OF THE VOYAGE, THE
LONGSHIPS SAILED INTO THE SETTING SUN
FOR ABOUT 875 KILOMETRES

GUNNAR SPOKE FLUENT GAELIC AND WAS
IN LONGSHIP NUMBER 5

13

LONGSHIP NUMBER 13 CARRIED ALL THE
WEAPONS AND 3 VIKING WARRIORS

VIKING ATTACK!

14

AFTER JULY 3rd, IN THE YEAR OF THE VIKING ATTACK, THE SUN WAS CONSTANTLY OBSCURED BY DARK CLOUDS EVERY DAY FOR 2 WEEKS

VIKING ATTACK!

15 LONGSHIPS LEFT OSLO ON SUNDAY
JUNE 15th

THORSKILD'S FATHER DIED AFTER A REIGN OF 16 YEARS

LONGSHIP NUMBER 12 ARRIVED
AT THE BATTLE SITE 2 DAYS AFTER LONGSHIP
NUMBER 10

FOR THE FIRST LEG OF THE VOYAGE THE LONGSHIPS SAILED DUE SOUTH FOR ABOUT 375 KILOMETRES

THE BATTLE COULD NOT TAKE PLACE UNTIL
AT LEAST 375 ARMED VIKINGS HAD ARRIVED
ON THE SITE

THORSKILD WAS 36 YEARS OLD
WHEN HE BECAME KING IN THE YEAR OF
HIS FATHER'S DEATH

FOR THE FOURTH LEG OF THE VOYAGE, THE LONGSHIPS SAILED IN A SOUTH-WESTERLY DIRECTION FOR ABOUT 250 KILOMETRES

LONGSHIPS NUMBER 8 AND 11 ARRIVED AT
THE BATTLE SITE 3 DAYS BEFORE LONGSHIP
NUMBER 4

EACH LONGSHIP HAD ENOUGH PROVISIONS
ON BOARD FOR 2 MONTHS AND 14 DAYS

VIKING SUPERSTITION AND FOLKLORE,
TO WHICH KING THORSKILD ADHERED RIGIDLY,
STATED THAT, IF IN ANY YEAR THERE WERE
MORE THAN 4 SUNDAYS IN THE MONTH OF
JUNE, THE 5th SUNDAY WOULD BE A DAY OF
PEACE WHEN NO VIOLENCE COULD BE
COMMITTED

VIKING ATTACK!

FOR THE THIRD LEG OF THE VOYAGE,
THE LONGSHIPS SAILED IN THE SAME DIRECTION
AS FOR THE FIRST LEG FOR ABOUT
1200 KILOMETRES

VIKING ATTACK!

THORSKILD'S FATHER BECAME KING OF
NORWAY IN 843 A.D.

VIKING ATTACK!

LONGSHIP NUMBER 3 ARRIVED AT THE
BATTLE SITE 16 DAYS AFTER LEAVING OSLO

VIKING ATTACK!

**THORSKILD
WAS KING OF NORWAY**

VIKING ATTACK!

LONGSHIPS NUMBER 1, 2 AND 5
TOOK 13 DAYS TO REACH THE BATTLE SITE
FROM OSLO

VIKING ATTACK!

THE ATTACK TOOK PLACE
ON THORSKILD'S 41st BIRTHDAY – THE FIRST
DAY ON WHICH ALL THE NECESSARY
CONDITIONS FOR BATTLE
WERE MET

VIKING ATTACK!

JULY 2nd
WAS A RELIGIOUS HOLIDAY
IN THE TIME OF KING THORSKILD

VIKING ATTACK!

THE VIKINGS IN LONGSHIP NUMBER 4 HAD PARTICIPATED IN THE SIEGE OF YORK SOME YEARS PREVIOUSLY

THE VIKING ATTACK TOOK PLACE AT ONE OF THESE LOCATIONS

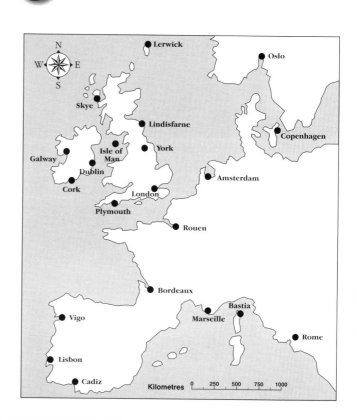

VIKING ATTACK!

VIKING ATTACK!
TIPS FOR TRAINERS

Here are some typical trends/tips/insights from the hundreds of groups who've solved the Viking Attack over the years.

- 8 out of 10 teams fail to listen to the Sunday in the June 15th departure from Oslo and, therefore, don't take it into account for their first calculation of the longship arrival schedule. They announce June 29th as the attack date – wrong! (Card 24 then allows them to calculate that June 29th was the 5th Sunday in June, hence no violence.)

- Once the map holder has announced that s/he has a map, you may want to allow that person to draw the route on the map (if you don't they probably will anyway!). Don't forget to make a new copy for your next course!

- Card 14 states that "After July 3rd the sun was obscured by dark clouds" ... This is a red herring (it's always raining in Rouen!) but it's amazing how many teams interpret it as meaning "no attack after July 3rd so therefore = July 2nd".

- Don't help teams when they're on the wrong track, it's part of the learning.

- Do tell them 'Yes' or 'No' when they announce a year, date or place to motivate them for the next step.

- The winning teams tend to work on one question at a time (the fastest teams always start with year) and discipline themselves to reading only those cards relevant to the question under discussion.

- The red herrings are cards numbers: 9, 12, 14, 31, 32.

ABOUT THE AUTHOR

John Townsend, BA MA MCIPD

John has built a reputation internationally as a leading trainer of trainers. He is the founder of the highly-regarded Master Trainer Institute, a *total learning* facility located just outside Geneva which draws trainers and facilitators from around the world. He set up the Institute after 30 years' experience in international consulting and human resource management positions in the UK, France, the United States and Switzerland.

From 1978–1984 he was European Director of Executive Development with GTE in Geneva with training responsibility for over 800 managers in some 15 countries. John has published a number of management and professional guides and regularly contributes articles to leading management and training journals.

In addition to training trainers, he is also a regular speaker at conferences and leadership seminars throughout Europe.

Contact

John Townsend, The Master Trainer Institute,
L'Avant Centre, 13 chemin du Levant, Ferney-Voltaire, France
Tel: (33) 450 42 84 16   Fax: (33) 450 40 57 37
www.mt-institute.com

THE MANAGEMENT POCKETBOOK SERIES

Pocketbooks

Appraisals
Assertiveness
Balance Sheet
Business Planning
Business Writing
Call Centre Customer Care
Career Transition
Challengers
Coaching
Communicator's
Competencies
Controlling Absenteeism
Creative Manager's
C.R.M.
Cross-cultural Business
Cultural Gaffes
Customer Service
Decision-making
Developing People
Discipline
Diversity
E-commerce
Emotional Intelligence

Employment Law
Empowerment
Energy and Well-being
Facilitator's
Handling Complaints
Icebreakers
Impact & Presence
Improving Efficiency
Improving Profitability
Induction
Influencing
International Trade
Interviewer's
I.T. Trainer's
Key Account Manager's
Leadership
Learner's
Manager's
Managing Budgets
Managing Cashflow
Managing Change
Managing Upwards
Managing Your Appraisal

Marketing
Meetings
Mentoring
Motivation
Negotiator's
Networking
NLP
Openers & Closers
People Manager's
Performance Management
Personal Success
Positive Mental Attitude
Presentations
Problem Behaviour
Problem Solving
Project Management
Quality
Resolving Conflict
Sales Excellence
Salesperson's
Self-managed Development
Starting In Management
Stress

Succeeding at Interviews
Teamworking
Telephone Skills
Telesales
Thinker's
Time Management
Trainer Standards
Trainer's
Training Evaluation
Training Needs Analysis
Vocal Skills

Pocketsquares

Great Training Robbery
Hook Your Audience

Pocketfiles

Trainer's Blue Pocketfile of
Ready-to-use Activities

Trainer's Green Pocketfile of
Ready-to-use Activities

Trainer's Red Pocketfile of
Ready-to-use Activities

ORDER FORM

Your details

Name _____

Position _____

Company _____

Address _____

_____

_____

Telephone _____

Facsimile _____

E-mail _____

VAT No. (EC companies) _____

Your Order Ref _____

Please send me:

No. copies

The   Trainer's Red Pocketfile _____ ☐

The _____ ☐

The _____ ☐

The _____ ☐

Order by Post

MANAGEMENT POCKETBOOKS LTD
LAUREL HOUSE, STATION APPROACH, ALRESFORD,
HAMPSHIRE SO24 9JH UK

Order by Phone, Fax or Internet

Telephone: +44 (0)1962 735573
Facsimile: +44 (0)1962 733637
E-mail: sales@pocketbook.co.uk
Web: www.pocketbook.co.uk

Customers in USA should contact:
Stylus Publishing, LLC, 22883 Quicksilver Drive,
Sterling, VA 20166-2012
Telephone: 703 661 1581 or 800 232 0223
Facsimile: 703 661 1501 E-mail: styluspub@aol.com

MANAGEMENT POCKETBOOKS